How To Be

The

SALESMAN

They

REMEMBER

How To Be

The
SALESMAN
They
REMEMBER

With special appendix:
"The Walt-isms"

Walt Atkins

To order additional copies of this book, contact:
Xlibris Corporation
1-888-795-4274
www.Xlibris.com
Orders@Xlibris.com
111742

Contents

Dedication

Dedicated to the memory of George Webb, a man of faith, to whom the author is indebted for the opportunity he gave to learn from him for three decades. Every salesman should have a leader like The Chief.

With special thanks to my wife Pam and our entire family, Jack Zane, Bob Savod, Bob Page, Parker Overton, Jerry Cooper, Ted Northrup, Ronny Pouncey, Dwayne Altice and a long list of loyal customers and friends whom God chorused into my life, always at just the right time.—WA

With a grateful heart to hundreds of skilled craftsmen and co-laborers it was a great pleasure to represent in the marketplace, as well as customers who became friends all across America.—WA

Part One

So you want a career in sales?

My hope is that by the time we finish you'll be enthusiastic about entering a career in sales or managing the sales for your company.

I had set my sights on a career in sports administration which I pursued for eight years until I decided to set aside my vow of poverty and go into sales. It was a good move. I would encourage you to get into sales if you possibly can.

A college professor friend of mine heard of my retirement and remarked that I must have learned something in 31 years. He asked me to tell his students about sales. Reflecting on his comment, I realized that I had indeed learned a few things.

Sales is a great profession. It is exciting. It is different. And, it's not for everybody! Do you have it in your heart to be a salesman? I hope you do. If you do, you will succeed. However, if you can be happy doing something else—then please do something else—because a career in sales is too demanding for the insecure or faint of heart! But if you have a burning desire in your heart to help people get what it is they want, to provide their needs, for them to be successful, then you should be in sales. If you must be doing those things, then climb aboard the sales train and enjoy an exciting life. You should be helping other people to get what it is they need.

Sales is the oldest and greatest profession, a most noble profession. It is the most important role in the economy today. Why? Because nothing happens in this country or your company until someone sells something! And then, that product has to be made or a service rendered in some fashion. It has to be delivered in the case of goods. That, too, requires vehicles and other things to be made. As a salesman, you are the hunter-gatherer of today's society. That's why I say it is the oldest profession. Burn it in—NOTHING happens in this country or your company until somebody sells something.

As a salesman you are the one shoveling the coal into the engine of your company. You ought to be revered by everyone in your company. (I'm not saying everyone should stand when you enter the room, but it would be a nice touch!) Are you willing to make more than the president of your company as some salesmen do? You can do it if you can sell! The president of the company is the last one to get paid, as most in business know. The salesmen get paid first.

And remember—you eat what you kill, just like that hunter-gatherer. That gives you the option to starve to death, but that's not really very satisfying. You won't like that for long. I used to think when I started in sales that sales was like a treadmill, you just have to keep walking. But I soon realized that it's more like the stair-stepper exercise machines, you must keep pumping hard or you sink!

You've got to be willing to invest your time and your talents in your customers and then you can be successful. There were two myths that people told me about sales. I was advised that the hours weren't bad and there was no heavy lifting! I can tell you after 31-non-stop years and making more than a few deliveries, in some cases heavy deliveries, that neither one of those is true!

Some readers will be planning to be entrepreneurs and own the company. Others may foresee a career in management, which might even include managing sales. Perhaps you are planning a career in sales even now. Some may even want to be accountants. Those are the people who nip at the heels of the salesmen! (Oops, my private joke. You'll understand by the end.)

I want to remind you about something Harvey MacKay said. He wrote *Swim With the Sharks Without Being Eaten Alive,* and many other business books and articles. I would recommend them all very highly. I have been through his company and have seen that what he says and does works well. Here's the story:

Harvey was on a business tour in the Orient some years ago and had explained his MacKay Envelope Company to his audience. At the end there was time for questions and answers. Harvey recognized a hand in the back:

"Harvey, how many employees do you have in your company?" the questioner asked.

"300," was Harvey's ready response.

"Oooh," went the crowd!

"Next question?" Harvey recognized another raised hand.

"That's impressive, Harvey," the listener said. "How many salesmen do you have?"

"300," Harvey shot right back.

Yes, everyone in his company and yours has to be conscious of sales, taking care of customers and meeting their needs every day! If everyone isn't doing that on a regular basis then you won't be in business, and they won't be working for you very long!

So now that we have made all of my readers honorary salesmen, let's pull back the veil and see what there is to selling—selling as a career. Regardless of which of those business careers you foresee for yourself, you must be conscious of sales for your company's long-term success and your role in it.

I can remember many days we had economic successes, made sales that were significant. That success was enjoyable, but in 31 years of selling, the personal memories outweigh the monetary ones. The people that you meet, the friendships that you develop, will be very important to you. They will be important to you personally and to your sales career. So making friends was an important part of the process for me.

The ability to research your customers and know them both personally and professionally, is an important skill for you. I will tell you that:

Customers don't care how much you know, once they know how much you care!

I've visited customers in hospitals and done other things because I cared for customers and their well-being and success. I didn't visit them to show that I cared, but because we did care. Caring has to be genuine. It was one of my favorite things to do, to be friends with our customers. Be sincerely interested in the people you meet.

Be interested in their success. As Zig Ziglar said, "Help enough other people get what they want, and you'll get what you want." I think that's important.

In college lectures we look at three aspects of sales:

The Company point of view, that of the owner/manager who depends on the sales force,

The Salesman point of view, where we will spend most of our time, and,

The Customer point of view, how they view the company and the salesman.

Let's get started.

Part Two

The Company Point of View

The job of hiring the salesman that you want around for a long time is the single toughest hire in business today.

I think of what Woody Hayes, the late Ohio State football coach, used to do when he needed to hire an assistant coach. Once he had identified the person he wanted to hire he would send them down the hall to meet his current assistant coaches. One-by-one they were interviewed by all the current position coaches. Coach Hayes told the candidate that he would later meet with his staff and ask each one their opinion of the potential new staff member. Then they would vote, and a unanimous vote was required. Make no mistake, the current assistants knew the boss approved of this candidate, but they also knew that he valued their insights and the unity of his staff. When the candidate got a call back and was offered the job, he knew he had the unanimous support of all the other assistants and the head coach. There would not be any back-biting or intramural rivalries, no one trying to show up the rookie.

Woody Hayes also said he always wanted to hire the right person for the job. He knew that he could teach all they needed to know about coaching the particular position that would be assigned. Printing, pharmaceutical, insurance and many other industries have a great deal of technical knowledge associated with them, but if you have hired the right person you, too, can teach them what they need to know about your business, and they can succeed.

You can easily see the consequences of your hiring actions. If you hire the wrong person, it won't make any difference what you teach them, because they won't follow through. They won't work to pursue success, ignoring the obstacles and seeing their effort all the way through to a successful conclusion on a daily basis. They might accept the first "No" and not come back. But if you hire the right person you can teach them what they need to know about your business and the market segment you serve. You can confidently send them out in the marketplace where they will succeed for you, finding potential customers who would benefit by working with your company.

As salesmen mature in the marketplace, they tend to develop relationships. Sometimes these candidates can bring particular accounts or a book of business with them to your company. Don't count too heavily on that because their former company is going to want to retain that business, too. Sometimes salesmen are available to change companies because their customers and the market have changed, but their current company can't adapt to the change. They have to move to continue helping their customers in this case.

On a personal note, when I arrived in early 1980, to the company from which I retired at the end of 2010, there were four printing presses, a single color, a two-color, a three-color web and the company's first four-color press. When I retired, 31-years later, there wasn't even a four-color press in the building any more. They had been replaced by two six-colors and two eight-colors, because that was what the customers required. The company had changed with the marketplace and I'm grateful that it did. In the beginning days the largest press was 40 inches wide, but in the end, 40 inches was the smallest press, with a 56 and a 64 taking over half the pressroom. Other equipment throughout the plant had been added as well to complement the gradual modernization that had taken place.

Had ownership not had the to vision to make those changes through the years, they would not have been able to do any of the work going on today. Every company has to keep up with the market or the salesmen might have to move to continue helping the customers.

Interview, discern their personal and work habits, check references and the social media, re-interview, let others interview your candidate, and make your decision. When you pull the trigger and make the hire, you have completed the first of the three-step process. Background checks, social media, drug testing and talking with people who know your candidates will help you to avoid hiring an alcoholic, a gambler, or worse. Character qualities are the most important. You can't teach character. A six-month evaluation period is sometimes compensated by a salary draw, particularly if the new hire is required to participate in training or other non-sales activities.

When you check references, be sure to consider the source. It might be difficult to talk with current employers. You could scuttle your candidate with their current employer if you do. A salesman might be in a position where a major client has a need which the current employer can't provide, or won't be able to provide in the future, so he is looking for the opportunity to continue helping that customer. The salesman isn't disloyal, just facing reality if the current company won't or can't adjust.

Here's the 3-Step process in successful Sales Hiring:

1—Hire the right person,
2—Teach them what you want them to know,
3—Give them the freedom to FAIL.

What did you say, Walt?

I'll explain it this way. I was talking with an athletic director at a major college. His football coach was getting some heat for not throwing passes to the tight end in his style of offense. The tight end is an extra blocker in most situations, but can be used as a receiver quite effectively from time to time.

The conversation went something like this:

"You're a wise old coach," I said. "You could take the young coach under your wing and let him benefit from your wisdom of years, couldn't you?"

"Yes, Walt, I could do that," said the senior leader, "But if I do that and he decides to use the tight end in his offense and it doesn't work and we lose, then I can't fire him, I have to fire me!"

The point was very clear at that moment. His coach had to have the freedom to fail.

The business application is that if you tell your salesmen who to call on and where to go and when—and it doesn't work—then who gets fired? Who should be fired? You'll know if your sales people are doing the right things because you will see the results. Sometimes sales volumes ebb and flow. In slow times, encourage your sales team to keep doing what they know is right. You are standing behind them and when the market is ready for what you do, they will get the results you need. Of course without sales, they will starve to death, but they will do so with you standing behind them!

Like the athletics director, don't micro-manage your sales team. It might not work as you hoped. Good salesmen will figure out how to add sales in a changing marketplace. If you prescribe too much and it doesn't work, it's difficult to fire him with a clean conscience. So keep that in mind as you hire people and put them out on the road for you. In certain companies, things like territories, reports and other elements are necessary, but be careful not to overload your salesman with unnecessary, unproductive things. You help them to focus on sales by taking as many burdens as possible off their backs. If your salesmen perform as we discuss In Part Three you will benefit greatly from his or her efforts for the long term.

As a personal aside, sometimes, people in our company would see me in the plant and comment, "Walt, I haven't seen you in a while."

"That's right," I would always respond. "Nobody in this building buys any printing! I'm not here to sell to you and you don't want to see me building a camp here. While I enjoy the fellowship and encouragement we give each other, you want me to be out with the customers. You need me to be out with the customers."

Be careful about demanding the physical presence of your salesmen. I'm not talking about being there with customers. By simply demanding some of their time in your office, you limit their opportunities with customers. Your salesmen aren't going to buy anything from you either, so let them be with customers and potential customers.

You, your outside salesmen and Donald Trump all have exactly the same amount of time in each day. Sometimes assignments or divisions of effort are necessary for efficiencies or expense reasons, but please be careful not to impose unnecessary, artificial boundaries on your sales team.

Some salesmen use the star system—Jacksonville Monday, Denver Tuesday, then Buffalo, Dallas, Minneapolis and back to Jacksonvile—you get the picture when you draw lines connecting those cities. You don't want that. You plan your work and work your plan back at the company—and you can encourage your sales team to do the same. They really don't want to do that either, but you can get caught in an unusual situation once in a while, too. As best you can, let the sales team manage their time and direction for their maximum success, which will lead to your best success.

If your product or service is regional, you might want to divide up potential customers by counties, for efficiency, and so your salesmen can be well-known in the marketplace. This particularly applies if you are supporting the team with general or targeted advertising in various media.

There are reasons to have territories, but even if someone is selling successfully in one territory, there may be one particular account that can't be cracked. You can send a different salesman into that single account if you deem it important to your company's success, but don't do it without talking with the current salesman in that territory. Perhaps two salesmen could make a trade, or double team accounts. You could show the elusive prospective customer how important they are by letting your salesman bring in your company president. I found it profitable to bring in other technical experts for support in the prospect's area of concern. Also look for others in your company who know the prospect.

Beware micromanagement. Time-consuming requirements like call reports, time sheets (a big no-no) and the like are largely counterproductive. Your salesmen are not on the clock—Except the 24-hour clock! (Remember that stair-stepper exercise machines we were talking about?)

There is only one report that actually matters in sales, the one at the end of the period (week, month, quarter, year or whatever cycle your company is on) that matters. It is the report of the volume of paid sales. Are you selling? How much are you selling? Are sales increasing?

Now you might say, but I need marketplace information to make plans for my company's future. Yes, you do. So ask your salesmen to report new information when they have it. They will. What benefit does a salesman receive by withholding valuable business marketplace information from his own company's leaders and decision makers? There's no value there. You both want to grow and be better able to serve clients for years to come. As I mentioned, by 2010 my former company looked a lot different from its founding in 1952 and from 1980 when I arrived—because it had changed to keep up with the marketplace. Where do you think management got the necessary information? In no small part from the sales team!

Some managers want to see a call list, who sales has seen and where they have been. If you need that information just ask to be told about what's going on in the marketplace. "Just tell me about it" would work fine, give you a better understanding and take up less time for both of you. Salesmen are your spies in the marketplace. Encourage your salesmen to come by and talk with you as their schedule allows. Ask them if there are ways that we can help you to grow your sales. You are talking with other business leaders in your industry or community, so you already know a lot, but it's nice to get some confirmation from the ground up, too.

Your salesmen are learning what the customer needs, what customers and prospects will be needing in the future, and, yes, even what your competitors are telling your customers about what they could provide in your place!

A final thought about paperwork. Be careful about overloading your sales team with paperwork, if you make the sales report sacred, you will have things showing up on the sales report that make the sales report look good, but that were counter-productive to your best interests. If you find that is happening, do away with that and just have them tell you what is going on in the marketplace.

Now we come to the compensation question. How are you going to compensate your sales people. That's why we have Rule #1. Whatever you reward you'll get more of and whatever you punish you'll get less of. It is Rule #1 for all of life, business and economy and is Walt-ism #1 (see the appendix). If you doubt me, just observe a mother in a grocery store with a two-year old. Whatever behavior she rewards, she will get more of. If she rewards whining she will get more whining.

If you reward hours, you will get hours. If you reward sales, you will get sales. As with most professional salesmen, having refused a monthly draw, I received absolutely nothing without a paid sale. Yes, not only did we have to make a sale, the customer had to pay for the product or service.

That's important. As a salesman you aren't out looking for customers who can't pay their bills. You're not looking for customers that would run from their bills, or dispute every invoice, or chisel your company either.

It is your accounting department's responsibility to do any financial background work your business requires, so as the owner, you have to make that happen. Once the corporate decision is made to do business with a given prospect, your company—not your salesman—should be responsible for the management of credit on the account. Keep the salesman informed so he can keep the customer informed. Professional salesmen know it is not in the customer's best interest to overextend, but it is not the salesman's fault if you neglect the financial oversight of your own business and become either too dependent on one customer or too at-risk because of one customer. Your salesman will assume all is well unless you tell him. Then he can work with the customer to maintain a proper business relationship for both of you.

A percentage sales commission is a good way to compensate your sales team and to control your balance sheet. A straight percentage on the gross is best. Let your sales team know in advance if anything doesn't count toward the commission. If you imbalance your percentage, which products or services do you think your sales team will sell? Yes, the ones that pay the most commission will be the items of focus. So plan well how you will compensate your salesmen. See Walt-ism #1.

Are you ready to go out and hire your sales staff?

Some companies like to start their salesmen on a draw, particularly right after having hired them and before you feel they know your business and your prospective customers well enough. You give them a while to warm up, so to speak. You can do that if you want to, but I feel it would be better to get them out on the road more quickly. I wouldn't recommend a draw unless you require non-sales activity. I certainly wouldn't recommend a draw for very long.

Get all the good salesmen that you can get. Major league managers want all the .300 hitters in the dugout that they can get. Hire all the good salesmen you can and support them all you can for your greatest success.

Part Three

The Life of a Salesman

Let's examine the *who, what, when, where, why and how* of being a salesman. I'm reverting to my journalism days for that phrase.

To begin with, ask yourself:

"What should I sell?"

Imagine you have never been a salesman, but you want to be one. You have a burning desire in your heart to succeed. But first you must decide what type of product or service you want to represent. My first advice would be to identify something expensive. Try to sell something for a higher dollar amount. A medical student was asked what his specialty would be and his response—diseases of the rich! Good answer.

Your product or service should have both a present need and a future in the marketplace. In a sense, your chosen product or service should have a moat, insurance that it will always have a position in the market. People will always eat, drive cars and do many other things you can think of—using products that people will always need. Technology is good, but be careful to make sure your prospect company is technologically advanced and advancing, not sitting on a product that will be replaced by something from another company that is bigger, faster, stronger, smarter, and perhaps less expensive than their's!

If you are looking at an office situation, is it up to date? The information technology, is it modern or outdated? Is there a debt load that would preclude modernization? For manufacturers on your radar screen, is the plant old and out of date or modern and hi-speed? Again, and particularly here, what is the debt load? If you find a company that is debt-free and modernized, as I did, you have a real opportunity there.

Where should I be employed? What company you represent is very important. What is the company's share in the marketplace today?

Investigate the companies that you are considering to help sell. Are they leaders or followers? Do they need help? What is their reputation and brand? For what are they known today? They should be viable in the marketplace. Their marketplace should have that moat, a defensible position for future growth. Can you increase their sales? Does the company stand behind its work? Is there a trail of praise or complaints in the social media about this company?

One of the things I was able to say repeatedly was that our company stands behind its work. That served us well over the years. I would remind our people in manufacturing, too, that we stand behind our work for our customers. We were able to retain business by standing behind our work.

Any company can do the job for your customer when all things are going along smoothly. You know you are working with the right company when things are in tumult and you make it right for your customer. Knowledge all across your company of this policy sharpens each individual's focus on quality and on-time performance. My particular business was custom manufacturing, making products exclusively for one purchaser. Marketing materials for one customer are of no interest to another. In commodity manufacturing, products can simply be replaced with others, but in custom manufacturing it is often not quite as simple.

After doing your research on what to sell and who to represent, ask yourself if that situation will help you reach your personal goals.

If you want to make as much money as possible, the best route is commissioned sales, but it can best be done only in the right situation.

If you position yourself high in the income stream for your company you will be rewarded handsomely for that. You can make money selling the symphony, airplanes, technology, printing, or almost anything—as long as you have the burning desire in your heart to succeed—and the right platform for your skills. Can you make money selling that chosen product or service in the market this year, the next and beyond? Before you decide, know the answers to those questions and know yourself. If you aim at nothing you'll hit it every time!

Who will buy from you? Are you entering a market that is business to business, or business to consumer, or business to consumer through distributors or other businesses? Figure out who it is that will buy from you. Very few people could buy the product I was selling. Though we see printing all the time, very few people buy printing. I'm talking about high volume commercial printing.

How do you evaluate your plan? Have you heard about those folks that thought they were in the buggy whip business? They were really in the transportation business, and just a small corner of it at that. Printing is a part of the communication and media business. Printing has to blend with and support internet, commercial media, social media and all forms of advertising. Printing companies that are not modernizing and incorporating cross-media are going out of business every week across America. Other businesses that don't keep up with the times will meet the same fate.

Once you are on the job, how will you evaluate your plan and performance? Start with your plan.

I believe in the Five Ps, Prior Planning Prevents Poor Performance. As some have said, Plan your work and work your plan. At least every year, step back from your plan and re-evaluate how that plan is working and what the plan needs to be for the next year. I call it re-inventing yourself. Do you need to re-focus in some particular way? Ask yourself if you are selling to the right customers, targeting the right prospects, and selling the right products and services. If you keep doing the same thing, will you keep growing your sales to maintain yourself and the company? Your plan will change and evolve. If you have a good plan, change won't be as drastic as to the bygone buggy whip business, but it will change.

It should be noted that you don't have to do anything wrong to lose 15% of your business each year. Things change rapidly in today's marketplace. Companies merge and move, including your customers. New people take over. Many things beyond your control will affect future opportunities. If you are likely to lose 15% of your business through natural causes, you must plan to grow your business by that amount each year or you will be going backwards.

I preferred evaluating my plan every six months. Once every year may be sufficient for you. The end of the year is often a good time to do that self-evaluation. I'm not talking about changing companies. You have already sold yourself on the business you represent and the products and services you sell. Evaluate how you do what you have committed to do. How can you do it better next year?

The byword in the market today is speed. Everything in business seems to be happening faster, needed faster, and changing faster. You must adjust to that. You must encourage your company to change to accommodate that. We used to live in a 30-minute society, with 30-second commercials. It only took 30 minutes to resolve any situation in a television program. Now it is an instantaneous resolution that most folks require.

Marketing departments today must respond quickly when they see competitors make special offers that change the playing field in their favor.

Your customers need you to be a rapid responder today because they can't let a competitor take market share while waiting on you to respond.

Now to the compensation question from your point of view. Commission is the best way to be paid. A straight commission on your sales is best.

You say you don't want to be on commission? It's too late! The dirty little secret is everyone is on commission!

If you are working store hours, carrying a business card, driving a company car on the road, taking insurance and making sales, a record is being established. If the value of your sales isn't up to the level of your draw, it won't be long before someone else is driving your car and taking that same draw. If you are in sales, you are on commission. Straight commission is the best way to go, from day one, if at all possible. The company furnishes the vehicle or pays your mileage, provides health insurance, and you eat what you kill. It's that simple with commission sales.

Vacation is a tricky thing. Under the scenario I just described you have no vacation. Vacation actually means paid vacation, and you don't get paid unless you sell, so you should negotiate for that benefit if you want it. Your status is somewhat in line with independent contractors in this regard. Perhaps you will be fortunate to join a company that issues vacation bonuses. Determine whether vacation bonuses, Christmas bonuses, annual bonuses, profit sharing, paid sick leave and the like are inside or outside your package. Establish and fund your own retirement plan as early as possible and as independently as possible. If you plan to lean on the government in retirement, you are leaning on a broken crutch. As respectfully as I can say it, your company may be compassionate, but it is not responsible for your lifetime income. You are.

Beware of hybrid compensation systems that have been installed to replace the commission method. Various forms of value-added compensation include payment for the dollars above the materials, or dollars above outside purchases, or dollars above some other established criteria. But make no mistake, these hybrid systems are not created to increase your compensation, so beware of those, particularly where variables are involved.

What do I mean by variables? What is the cost of materials in your manufacturing process? Is it the invoice from the supplier? What if the supplier rebates a percentage based on annual purchases? What if the purchase was financed? The amount can be wildly different if too many variables come into play. Again, hybrid commission systems are not designed to increase your compensation.

Have it determined how you will be paid prior to beginning sales. I would recommend a straight commission figured from the gross. Your company wants more top line billing and so do you. This aligns the goals for both. The higher the top line billing, the more the company has to work with to perform for customers.

Develop your goal, your strategy, and your tactics. Your career success depends on these. Don't just wing it!

You must have a goal. So, what is your goal as a salesman?

You goal is to make money, of course!

You want to make money and you want your company to make money! If your company goes out of business, it's not likely that you will make any money there the next year. Picking the right customers is similarly important when we get to Part Four. You'll have a lot of trouble getting re-orders from customers who go out of business.

You should develop your strategy, a simple method to follow for sales success. What is your sales strategy?

Your strategy is to maximize revenue from satisfied customers.

Some folks hear that and think the first part is the more important. It is the second part that is more important. Satisfied customers will maximize revenue for you, with more orders, referrals and prompt payments. If you don't believe me, just try to get repeat orders and referrals from dissatisfied customers!

The application of my strategy included looking for orders that were $50,000 and above. Why? In manufacturing it takes just as many job jackets, proofs or prototypes to produce a $5,000 order as it does a $50,000 order or a $200,000 order. It takes just as much face time or attention to detail as well. The larger order just has more manufacturing time in it.

While that work is happening you can be selling something else. Consider that ten $5,000 orders would equal one $50,000 order, but would involve more handling by your inside customer service, your scheduler and traffic departments, and very likely there would be conflicting deadlines in a bouquet of jobs that large. With larger orders there is more money on the top line for the company to work with and grow, more commission for the salesman, and it is a better use of your time.

Yes, you will get some $2,000 and $5,000 jobs from your customers, and you will take very good care of them. But you aren't looking for the small orders.

Climb the mountain, as high as you can. The higher you climb the mountain, the clearer the air, the farther you can see and the less competition you will encounter. At the lower dollar level, there is easier entry into your marketplace by competitors. Remember the moat we talked about earlier? If your company can perform at a high level, that is, a high dollar level, the more difficult it will be for others to compete with you.

Burn it in, satisfied customers are the key to professional sales (Walt-ism #16).

Develop effective tactics as a professional salesman. My tactic was to emphasize personal contact with projects, their owners and their buyers. Sometimes the buyer and the owner are not the same. The owner—the creator, the mother of the baby—has certain goals and expectations for their projects. Sometimes the buyer has different goals. Be sure you know who signs the check so to speak.

Involve others as much as possible. As a part of the personal contact concept, I always tried to involve as many people in our company as appropriate in the relationship with the customer. This means customer service, manufacturing personnel, ownership and management. I wanted our two companies to bond at as many levels as possible. I wanted customers to know the people who actually did the work for them. I especially wanted our people to see the customer, personally, in their mind's eye whenever they worked on every project. I wanted the customer and my company's employee to talk shop. They could get in each other's heads, find the same wave length, and understand each other and the needs of the project better.

If your support employees ever come to view each new order as just being more work, you are dead as a company—if not now, soon. If your support personnel know the customer and are grateful for their work, then they will take greater pride in the work and the customer will have more confidence in your company.

When a problem arises during your order process, if the customer knows the skill and dedication of your people, the customer will be more likely to listen attentively as you describe the situation and present options for what needs to be done.

Why will they give you the benefit of the doubt if a problem arises? Because the customer knows that your company and its people understand what they need. If you can get to that kind of relationship you will have business for a long time. Your company will also have business after you retire if you connect at several levels with customers.

Make sure the customers who visit your offices meet several people, perhaps the president of the company. The president will automatically express thanks to the customer for their business. Others should be encouraged to do the same thing. Your customers are wonderful people, they pay all your bills! They put your children through college! These are wonderful people indeed.

Let your support staff know who they will see or be meeting and why it is important. Your best employees will see the value of this immediately. Make it a point to thank your people later when your customer tells you they enjoyed meeting one of them or reports to you on a conversation with one of your people.

Don't hover over your staff and the customer. Let them know that you trust them both to have a conversation on their own.

If there are areas into which the customer can not go for security, confidentiality or safety reasons, please say so in advance. If the reason is confidentiality, first mention that you have never allowed other customers to see their work in process, and so you honor them with the same standard. This is not common, but if you produce a product in general use across a marketplace, it is possible, so be aware of that.

As much as possible get some of the minutia and even paperwork transferred to others inside the company. That will benefit everyone and give you more time with customers and prospective customers. You want customers to rely on you, but you don't have to be the only one to call with every single question that arises. Just be sure that the right person calls with the questions and that you are notified of the event. If you walk in 30 minutes later and ask the same question, the customer might wonder if you two talk. Internal communication is vital.

I jokingly told my customer service representatives that I could look stupid enough on my own without any help. If there is delay in furnishing information to you, that delay could allow you to contact a customer and fall into a pothole. Some in your own company might think you are sloughing off by asking them to call customers, but your motivation is to involve them in the process, too. You are in the marketplace, seeing more customers—and that is what they really need for you to be doing, even if they don't realize it yet.

Knowing as many people as possible at your customer's company is important to your long-term success. I remember the day I called one customer to firm-up the time for our appointment that afternoon, only to be told, "I'm sorry Walt, Mr. Jones died last night." That was one of those moments that suck all the oxygen out of the room. I expressed my regrets and followed up at an appropriate interval. If I had not known several other people in that company we might not have continued doing business with them as we did through my retirement.

Knowing and being known by as many faces and names is also good because people at each customer will change position or responsibility from time to time. They may move to other companies, start new companies, or in some other way allow you to grow your customer base and sales network.

Also know the person who controls the schedule of your customer or prospect. The gatekeepers can be your helpers as well. Some assistants will be bosses somewhere else one day.

Knowing as many people in your customer's company is key to your long-term success.

You must work to know the marketplace. Be on the lookout for vital business information for your company. When we were talking earlier about bringing that vital business information to your company, it comes into play here. You are not trying to change your company into something it isn't! Here's what I mean.

One day all the salesmen were gathered and had the attention of the President of a company. He listened patiently as one after another commented that if the company only could do one additional thing or another, that sales could be bigger. The President returned an emphatic response that abruptly ended the discussion: "Will you please sell something that we do!" So bringing marketplace information back to your company doesn't mean trying to change the company.

There is plenty of business for your company as it is today. You have already determined that you have the right products or services for the marketplace and that you are representing the right company, so stop whining and go and do it! Don't try to change your company into something it isn't, but be ready with vital information to keep your company on the right track for the future.

Technology is changing business today. Stay on top of it. Manufacturing, information systems, service industries, the entire marketplace is on the move, so be ready for change to happen. It used to happen slowly, but now it happens very fast. If your company is like most, you will observe that every piece of hardware and software that you acquire is bigger, faster, stronger and smarter than whatever it replaced, if there was anything there before it arrived.

Business owners must be ready to move quickly. One company president I knew told me he didn't want to be the first to try any new thing, but once it was ready for the marketplace he didn't want to be any later than second. He said he wanted to be on the cutting edge of technology, but not on the bleeding edge. As salesmen, you can assist your company in this effort.

By now, if you are still reading, I hope you are excited about being a salesman. It is a wonderful opportunity. You get to help people get what they need, and you get paid for it! It's quite a racket. You don't have to invest in your company, and you don't have any risk. Your customers will pay your bills for you—buy your house, educate your children, put food on your table—and you didn't even take the risk. The owner of the company is going to take all the risk and pay you handsomely for making the owner rich!

How does the marketplace perceive and receive you? Be the same person wherever you are. If you visit a prospect and find that he is a Yankee fan, but you happen to be a Red Sox fan, don't become a Yankee fan. He'll see right through that before too long. Let him talk about the Yankees. He's the one who loves the Yankees! Be who you are. Your character can't change with the environment.

Customers and prospects all have different needs or styles though. Some are more business-like, others family oriented, or conversationalists, so you can adjust the conversation to the circumstances, but always be yourself, what you are. If the customer or prospect enjoys talking about grandchildren and you have grandchildren you can participate in that conversation. Sometimes you can detect their interests by surveying their office. Find out what interests your customers. The things that interest my friends interest me.

You will rapidly develop a reputation in your marketplace. So, what is your brand? From the customer's point of view you are known for something. It is the thing that distinguishes you from the man who just left and the woman sitting in the lobby waiting to come in. Are you the one with the best products, or best service, or the most unique answers to problems, or the nearest, or smartest, or something else. Please don't be known as the one who is always 15 minutes late! If you can't be on time, how will customers have confidence that your products or services will be timely? I liked to be known for delivering a little more than I promised. I called it "putting a little sugar on top." Here's one example:

I worked with some customers who created maps. When the order was complete I would have a couple dozen flat maps film laminated. I put grommets in the corners so they could easily be hung in the office. Customers loved those special maps. They weren't in the contract. We did it to add value. I would even tell them we wanted to "put a little sugar on top." Customers really felt special being able to please their bosses, co-workers and friends with something extra. I made sure to give them enough to be free with handing them out! It didn't cost, it paid!

Do you remember that we said your customers don't care how much you know once they know how much you care? They will bring you their problems and concerns once they trust you. When you hear one of your customers say, "The boss is really after me to solve this problem and I don't know what to do," you will know they trust you.

Maybe I had one of those faces, but people used to tell me their situation more often than I can count. You have the opportunity to solve problems for customers. You might brainstorm it right there, but you can also come back (very soon) with options once you have had time to think about it and apply all you know. You might have a solution your company can provide, or even suggest something you can't provide—but be sure you have their best interests in view when you give that counsel. You are willing to become an unpaid consultant at times. People will remember who helped them with their problems.

Be confident in what you know but don't fake it. If you don't know, you can always say, "I know someone at our company who does know the answer and I'll get it for you. I don't know yet, but I will know the answer." That can also give you another opportunity to return for a visit. "I'll have the answer for you on Friday," you might say. And then bring them the answer on Thursday.

What's your elevator speech? How do you explain in one or two sentences what your company does that is beneficial to your listener? In the time that you ride on an elevator you should be able to paint a clear picture of what your company does.

If you don't have the business you want yet, be in line to get the business. Be in as many lines as you can. Invest in those prospects. You never know what might happen. Maybe the customer will retire or get fired and a new face will be buying for the prospect. Maybe the current #1 salesman will retire, or die, get arrested, or move to another state far away, or his company will be acquired or close.

You be ready when a change in the marketplace happens. Be an observant follower of that target company and express your interest, love and concern for them and their desire to be successful. Be ready to take up the slack so they don't miss a beat.

Customers want more and more and more these days. The traditional three-legged stool of quality, price and service is no more. Customers want more quality, better service and better pricing, sometimes unreasonably better pricing. You have to deliver value.

Everyone can delivery quality these days. That's taken for granted today. If you deliver an inferior product, you won't be in business very long. People are getting more conscious of the dollar, so help them to spend their dollars better. Deliver full value for their investment.

If your product is insurance, sell the type of insurance that the client needs in the amount that they need and stay in contact because those needs are going to change. Be ready with good solutions.

Sometimes customers or prospects want unreasonable prices. If their budget is below their needs, devise something that is within their budget that still meets the need.

In this e-commerce environment, some customers get the idea that they don't want a salesman, they just want to buy the product. Oooh, that's a bad mistake in many cases. Customers need an expert to guide them through most purchases today or they will be susceptible to making the wrong buying decision. If something goes wrong, they will need an advocate within your company—which stands behind its products and services—as you remember. As a professional salesman you're not afraid to tell your own company that it made a mistake, that the customer is disappointed in some way. You will help correct the problem with the invoice or the product, or whatever the problem is. We made a boo-boo. We injured our customer in some way. We have to make it up to them. Do you remember we talked about how any supplier will do when things are going smoothly? Customers know they are working with the right company when things aren't going smoothly and you—along with your company—respond in a way to make it right for them. By the way, it is very important to get agreement on the problem first. Then get agreement on the solution. Then carry out the solution knowing the result going forward will be an improved relationship, not a broken one.

Tell all of your people that when they see you or any of your company's salesmen, to imagine that they are seeing a customer. I didn't buy any printing either, but I represented those who did buy from us!

Keep customers informed. Sometimes they have unreasonable expectations and you can meet them, but not always. But if you prevent them from being surprised in a bad way or disappointed, it will be better for all. If a customer's boss walks in to their office and asks about a particular project for which you are the vendor, the worst thing that can happen is for them to respond that they don't know. You have allowed your customer to be embarrassed and disappoint his boss. That's bad luck.

Sometimes you misinform a customer. If you do, get right back to them with the correct information and apologize for your mistake.

Your customer has to trust you. If you tell them the truth, you don't have to remember what you told this customer and what you told the other.

Part Four

Identifying customers

It's rather like being in school. You can grade your customers, A-B-C-D-F. Sound familiar? And guess what, you will likely have some in all categories! Turn your searchlight on the market to find the best customers for you.

Here's a three-legged stool of customer evaluation:

Volume
Profitability
Frequency

Volume is pretty easy to understand. This customer gives you a lot of work. This may or may not be your #1 customer in total volume. Since you will have several of these, they can't all be #1. Bring it on. We want all we can get!

Profitability is also easy to understand, but not as easy to define. If you are buying $100,000 of materials and selling a finished product for $80,000 you aren't profitable, that's obvious. Some customers value the products and services they receive from you more than others and will pay-up for the valuable work you do. Some put a high value on it or want to be important to you since you provide such a vital part of their business. Others want to pay as little as possible and shop their business around while demonstrating no loyalty to you. You may see some customers actually try to grind you down. Buyers should get what they pay for and should pay for what they get. You will be asked for your very best from these customers.

Frequency means you receive work each week, month or season for that customer. These are accounts not jobs. Frequently orders are followed by re-orders and as long as you treat the customer fairly and provide top-notch products and services, they won't be too fussy about what you charge—as long as it's fair. Don't abuse this relationship even one time. You are the trusted resource who will perform miracles for this customer when needed. Customers in retail sales are particularly good for the continuous flow of business.

So there is your **"A" customer**, large orders of profitable business frequently received.

That's great! Guess what? Your competitors want those customers, too and will work to get them away from you, or to share the business with you. You must service them well and you will!

Then there is the **"B" customer**. He's missing one of those legs. For example, this customer gives you a really big order, it's profitable to be sure, but it only happens once a year. If this is the case you will need to have similar customers at other times of the year.

Or, this "B" customer presents you with small, profitable orders on a regular basis. The annual total is good enough to keep your interest, but you want more. This customer also prevents you from having a blank month between large orders by "A" customers! This work fits well around other work, usually moves to the front of the line, and you are glad to have it. Your plant manager loves to have an even flow of work with less idle time.

Or, this "B" customer presents you with a steady stream of orders with a smaller profit margin. This customer may allow you to be a better buyer of your raw materials for all customers and have a positive effect on cash flow. If you handle this lower-profit work you will be seeing the customer on a daily basis and may be in line for bigger orders. Maybe you can help this one become an "A" someday.

Then there is the **"C" customer**. This customer is missing two of the three legs. You still want this business because the one leg is very strong. The order is either high volume, or profitable or frequent, but is only one of the three. You might be able to help this customer add another leg as time goes on. This customer could also be one who levels out the work in your plant, but you see that this one has real potential for growth.

Then there is the "D" customer. Why are you working with that firm? You're working with him because your "A" customer said, "Would you please help my friend over at this other company. He could really use your help." As a favor to your "A" customer you will work with this friend of his. You will try to see if you can move him up the grade scale in some way, so he will become a good customer, worthy of your time and attention. But if not, work with him anyway, at least for a while, because Mr. Big asked you to work with him. You can offer to introduce him to someone better suited to his needs. Because of your relationship with your "A" customer you can explain the situation to him that his friend can best be served in another way. Continuing to service the "D" customer when you have determined you can't help him will require time that will take away time from your "A" customer and others. Hopefully these customers will be professional and understand that you are helping him by putting him in contact with the proper segment of your market. Remind "A" you need more time on his orders if that is true.

And, how about the **"F" customer**? Who is that, and why are you working with them? Guess how many legs they have? None! And no hope of ever growing legs! But your spouse will divorce you if you don't do your brother-in-law's work. You may encounter a few of these during your career—that have no prospect of ever being anything that will help you and your company to meet your goals. Hopefully you won't get attached to many.

Try to have as many "A" customers as you can, have some "B" and "C" customers and remember the old 80/20 rule. A-B-C-D-F is the rank and the 20 percent that delivers 80 percent of your sales will come from the top ranks of customers. That's where you want to be concentrating to meet your company's goals and your own. Find an "A", develop an "A" customer and you will be well served for the long term.

Another concept to remember is LTV, the life time value of a customer. The "B" or "C" customer likely has merit in this measure. You are well suited to do their work. The customer loves you and your product or service or location. Their work rolls in and your whole team knows what to do to satisfy the customer. It's not quite on auto-pilot, but after a few rounds, you touch it less and your support team touches it more. They are so loyal and they will put money in your pocket every year. They are so valuable. Some of these customers fly below the commercial radar. Your competitors may not notice them. If you service them well this customer won't go looking for an alternative.

Sales and accounts are different. Accounts will carry you further than single sales. A one-time order is a sale. A customer with lots of orders is an account. This is pretty obvious to most, but early in your career you might be fooled by some customers who wish to appear more important than they are. Focusing on the LTV that an account offers can be a help here. Accounts often have more than one department or program or region where they can use your expertise. If you gain their trust in one aspect of their business you may be able to gain it for other areas as well.

The areas we discussed for evaluating customers are viewed and evaluated differently by the others in your organization. In the sales department, you like the big paycheck that follows the big order. The accountant looks at profitability. Manufacturing likes a steady flow of work without peaks or idle time. The company president likes the certainty of guaranteed future income that comes with a long term contract when your bank is considering a loan.

Accounting's determination of profitability involves variable calculations that can be used to prove or disprove almost any evaluation. Here's a shocker—From my observation of custom manufacturing, we have never, ever produced a profitable job! Walt! That's crazy you say! Complete the thought.

Here's my reasoning. Most companies never produce a profitable order—at the exclusion of all the other orders in the plant! Here's why:

Does your company sell a single order that pays all the bills, salaries, taxes and expenses for a whole year—without being combined with all the other orders? While a big order is in one department, something else has to be in all the other departments and when that biggie moves through production to other departments something has to replace it at the front end. You will likely never have one order that is so profitable that you won't need all the other orders your company receives to make your company profitable. It all fits together to make you profitable in the big picture.

I say this to make you aware that there are factors of profitability that are not measurable by your accountant. Of course, you must identify the materials costs and sell well beyond that, but you may have to identify additional benefits to the company if your accountant tries to create doubt. Long term contracts that ownership likes are sometimes difficult for cost accountants to evaluate accurately. Also, beware someone trying to explain to you that an order is not profitable if you know it is being billed at market prices. If other successful companies of your type in the marketplace are willing to provide the same work for the same price, you are at the market level. Draw some satisfaction from the wisdom of others. Hold onto the truth you know. It is an important part of the full basket of orders your company receives.

Your integrity is also important here. If you determine that a customer's work can not be produced at a profit, it is in your best interest to find another customer, because you want your company to be around for the long term, not to go under because some segment of work was unprofitable and dragged down the profitable work. Sometime the marketplace will only value certain products in your basket at certain levels, but you have to provide the full palate of insurance, or auto service or manufactured products. It all fits together, but be careful to manage your sales for the long-term benefit of you and your company.

If you doubt me on this evaluation of accounting I would refer you to Eliyhu M. Goldratt, author of *The Goal,* which exposes cost accounting and explains the theory of constraints in manufacturing. Everyone you work with may not like every order you secure for your company, particularly if they have lost sight of the need for sales and just consider everything that comes in the door to be more work (Oh, No!).

So when you are out looking for "A" customers, look for customers that have money, preferably lots of money. You can not sell to someone who doesn't have any money. I'm pretty sure that's true. And when you find an "A", put your shovel into the pile and dig all the way through the mountain. Aim high. Plan your work and work your plan. Remember, if you aim at nothing you will hit it every time!

Part Five

Bonus thoughts . . .

Which is the best personal organizer? The answer: The one you will use! You can have the fanciest forms or electronic gizmos, but if you won't use them they won't help you. Find one you can understand and use it faithfully.

Enter your orders as completely as possible. It makes things more efficient to your support team, enabling them to satisfy the customer more promptly than if they have to keep checking with you or the customer for minor details. Touch your orders as few times as possible yourself. Your time is valuable to you and your customers. If your support staff doesn't have time to do it right, when will there be time to do it twice?

Never make a cold call. Always be introduced. This is another concept I learned from Harvey MacKay. This can be formal or informal or even something you can create while talking with a prospect. "I was talking with a mutual friend (whom you then name) the other day," you might say. "And your name came up." Already he likely feels warmer toward you—if he likes the person you mentioned.

Voicemail, e-mail and gatekeepers can be your friends. Make friends of your customers and their people. I identified a series of projects in Vermont that I thought were well suited for my former company to be able to benefit a company there, and was talking with the prospect about the work. We had several conversations over the phone and one day I told him that I would try to work it out to come see him and preview the next project. I could hear him rolling his eyes from all the way down in North Carolina. Two weeks later we spoke and I told him that I had worked it out to come see him and gave him the date. Being off the beaten path, this customer was not used to having vendors call on him very often. He was surprised and very happy. We did his work for several years before the local companies figured out what happened and revised their facilities to service his needs there.

I once visited a customer and was told that she hadn't been called on by a printer in 11 years! I told her that on behalf of the entire printing industry, I apologized, and promised that she would get personal service from me. She did because we got her order that day.

It counts for a lot when you are willing to go visit people so both of you can put faces with names. Don't just be the guy on the phone. In this day of emails and the cell phone, it is still a live person, with feelings, who places the orders and pays the invoices. A machine is not going to do it. Know those people and be known to them. Put things on a friend basis as you talk to them. Make it easy for them to remember you, personally, even if they don't see you but a few times a year. It will elevate the conversation.

Any occasion when the customer won't identify who is in charge is a problem for you. One person is trying to give instructions and another is giving instructions and those instructions conflict. You have to stop that. You must identify who is the one who is going to write the check at the end. If it's their money, they get to decide.

Don't leave customers with any lingering uncertainty. You are to provide solutions, not problems. You will offer options, but don't offer confusion. If you don't know the answer to a question, get right back to the customer as quickly as you can with the answer. It bears repeating, one of the worst things you can have happen is for your customer's boss to walk in and ask about the project you are handling for their company. Your contact is supposed to know and keep the boss informed, but responds that he doesn't know. Ouch! You have embarrassed your contact in front of his boss. It will take a long time to overcome that mistake.

Sometimes you attempt and achieve difficult things for your customers. You might make it look so easy they think anyone can do it. Your competitors may even think they can do it, too. You must let the customer know what a great job you have done. Sometimes you have to tell them the impossible situation that arose and that you solved it. With all your magical powers—your fingers never left your hand—you provided the needed solution. I call it the Proverbs 32:1 principle. Except one tooteth their own horn, by whom shall it be tooted? (Walt-ism #12)

A sales career might mean some time away from home. When I retired, Marriott told me that I had spent over 1,000 nights in their care over 31 years. One of my map customers took the mileage that I had put on company cars during that same time and calculated that I had been completely around the globe. He actually discovered that I had driven around the equator the equivalent of 39 times in those 31 years. Seeing those customers may mean time on the road, but it will be worth it. It pays off in the long run.

Set high standards for yourself.

Be sure to be complimentary. Be sure to say thank you. We often wait until the funeral to say we love someone. Don't wait to express your thanks and do it often. Time is short and eternity is long. May your success be abundant, your problems few and your relationship with God secure. Remember to say "thank you" and "I love you" while you can.

If you have a passion for helping others achieve their goals and are driven to succeed, then a career in sales is for you. Aim high!

"Walt-isms"

1 — Whatever you reward, you'll get more of. Whatever you punish you'll get less of. (This is the #1 rule of all of life, business and economy. Need proof, just observe a mother with a two-year-old in the grocery store!)

2 — Work expands to fill the time alotted. (a.k.a. the Last Cookie Principle)

3 — You do not get what you expect, you get what you inspect. (Most things you inspect will be right, but don't be discouraged or stop, because if you do not inspect at all, something will be wrong.)

4 — Many folks today know the cost of everything and the value of nothing!

5 — Sometimes it's dangerous to pay too little!

6 — If there isn't time to do it right, when will there be time to do it twice?

7 — National Warehouse Motto: No aisle is so wide it can not be blocked.

8 — Sometimes we make things look so easy, customers think anyone can do it. (See #12.)

9 — The mind, once expanded by a new idea, never returns to its former size.

10 — The person who does not read is no better off than the person who can not read.

11 — Effective advertising and marketing materials are inexpensive, but products that don't do the job are expensive at any price. (Smart marketers are looking for all the good advertising they can buy!)

12 — Proverbs 32:1, Except one tooteth their own horn, by whom shall it be tooted? (See #8.)

13 — The bitterness of poor product quality or service or late delivery is remembered long after the sweetness of low price is forgotten.

14 — Exceed customer expectations the first three times and they will value doing business with you. Then continue to exceed their expectations.

15 — Whoever rides a tiger can never dismount.

16 — Satisfied customers are the key to professional sales.

17 — Make sure to order enough the first time because it's the first one that costs you, the rest are free. (That's not quite true, but it's a lot closer than novice buyers think. To test it, just order a reprint or re-supply if you come up a little short.) A customer and friend recently repeated this back to me, remembering it from 15 years earlier!

18 — Success in life is . . . finding God's Will for your life and following it.

19 — Prior Planning Prevents Poor Performance.

20 — Sales is a way of life, but it is not life itself.

The Author

Walt Atkins, Graham, NC
Maryland '72, BS Journalism

"Sales is a way of life, but it is not life itself."
"Success is finding God's Will for your life and following it."

After graduation from Maryland, Walt served as Assistant Sports Information Director at NC State University in Raleigh, NC for six years and two years as Sports Information Director at East Carolina University in Greenville, NC. Walt shifted to a sales career March 10, 1980 and retired December 31, 2010. He and his wife Pam reside in Graham, NC, where they work together on their investments, enjoy their ministries, family, golf and travel. Their daughter Cristy and her husband Thomas Slawson, are Christian missionaries to Russia. Walt and Pam have four grandchildren, two of whom have already been promoted to Heaven. Both are active Sunday School teachers at Beacon Baptist Church in Burlington, NC. Walt has earned a private pilot's license and served two elected four-year terms on the Graham City Council.

Walt Atkins
414 Ridgecrest Dr.
Graham, NC 27253   336-263-7677
walt@netpath.net   www.waltatkins.com

Desire personal sales coaching?

Contact Walt Atkins to discuss a program suited to your needs:

414 Ridgecrest Dr.,
Graham, NC 27253
walt@netpath.net 336-263-7677
www.waltatkins.com

Walt Atkins has limited availability for undergraduate and graduate business and marketing classes. Use the contacts above.